The Story of
CONFUCIUS I

www.royalcollins.com

Picture Story Book of Ancient Chinese Thinkers

The Story of CONFUCIUS I

Guo Defu

Translated by Wu Meilian

Books Beyond Boundaries

ROYAL COLLINS

Picture Story Books of Ancient Chinese Thinkers
The Story of CONFUCIUS I

Guo Defu
Translated by Wu Meilian

First published in 2024 by Royal Collins Publishing Group Inc.
Groupe Publication Royal Collins Inc.
550-555 boul. René-Lévesque O Montréal (Québec) H2Z1B1 Canada

ISBN: 979-8-9852490-2-6

To find out more about our publications, please visit www.royalcollins.com.

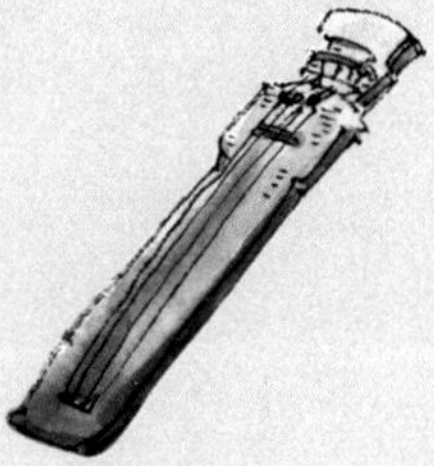

From a little child to a young man coming of age, from the middle-aged years of bustling activity to old age spent in scholarly pursuits, these ordinary yet heartwarming moments of family life and familial love, these stories of perseverance and steadfast seeking despite hardships—all vividly portrayed on paper.

The artist follows in Confucius's footsteps, tirelessly pursuing and sketching a true-to-life image of Confucius, allowing people to enter Confucius's world in a more intimate way.

On September 28, 551 BCE, a healthy boy was born at Mount Ni, Changping Xiang, Zouyi (southeast of today's Qufu, Shandong Province). He was the son of the brave and powerful warrior Shuliang He of the State of Lu and his wife, Yan Zhengzai.

The happy couple named the boy Kong Qiu, with the courtesy name Zhongni, after Mount Ni. Kong Qiu's father, who was then mayor of Zouyi and an old man, loved his son very much. The loving parents took good care of their little boy and planted the seed of love in his heart as he grew up.

When Kong Qiu was three, his father passed away, and his mother was left to support the family by herself. She and her young son moved to Queli in the city of Qufu, where she struggled to make ends meet by doing laundry and working in the fields.

Despite all the hardships, Yan Zhengzai never gave up on Kong Qiu's education. Her diligence, tenacity, kindness, and devotion to learning left a life-long impact on Kong Qiu.

According to the *Examination of the Confucius Family*, Yan Zhengzai insisted on buying ritual objects for Kong Qiu as toys and encouraged him to learn and observe etiquette even in the most difficult times. Kong Qiu became interested in sacrificial ceremonies when he was only five or six, and he often imitated adults to perform all kinds of sacrificial rituals.

Yan Zhengzai placed great emphasis on Kong Qiu's virtue education. Aside from teaching him to read and write, she often told him heroic stories of his father, Shuliang He, who had fought for the State of Lu many times. Once, he led three hundred soldiers, fought through a siege, saved Zang Wuzhong, the minister of Lu, and defeated the enemy.

Following his mother's guidance, Kong Qiu developed a strong passion for knowledge as he grew up and became well-known for his erudition at a young age. Later, when he looked back on his life, he said, "At fifteen, I had my mind bent on learning."

Kong Qiu's mother passed away when he was seventeen. He took pains to find his father's grave and buried his parents together at Mount Fang, east of Qufu.

During his mourning period, Kong Qiu heard of a banquet for local scholar-officials held by the high minister Jisun, and he attended as the county mayor's son.

However, Jisun's retainer, Yang Hu, rejected Kong Qiu at the door, saying, "My lord invited scholar-officials, not you." It was Kong Qiu's first time to know the hard truth about wealth and power.

Kong Qiu was always eager to learn, and he often sought advice from knowledgeable people. Some said, "Who says the mayor's son is courteous? He asks about everything."

When Kong Qiu heard, he said, "You ask when you don't know something; that is courtesy."

There was a ceremonial tilting vessel called *qiqi* (tilting vessel) in the Imperial Ancestral Temple. It only stayed upright when it contained the right amount of water and would automatically overturn and spill its content once it was full. The *qiqi* was placed on the right-hand side of the king's throne to remind him of the principle "pride causes harm, modesty receives benefit," which Kong Qiu also learned from it.

When he was nineteen, Kong Qiu married Qiguan from the State of Song. The next year, his son was born. Kong Qiu named him Li (carp), with the courtesy name Boyu (fish), to commemorate the honorable present of a carp given by Duke Zhao of Lu.

Since he lost his father at a young age, Kong Qiu treasured his time with his son very much, and he enjoyed playing with his family in the snow in winter.

The first job Kong Qiu had after he married was to manage the granary for Jisun, the Lu Minister. Despite its insignificance, he was very dedicated to his position and carefully recorded transactions. Later, he was appointed to be a manager of husbandry, which he also treated responsibly.

When he took care of the cows and sheep, he carefully observed and followed their natural instincts so that they could grow well. When the animals ate and played, Kong Qiu accompanied them with music.

When Kong Qiu was twenty-seven years old, he learned the zither with the famous musician Master Shi Xiang. After half a month, Master Shi Xiang advised him to learn a new piece, but Kong Qiu said, "I have yet to grasp the essence of the one I'm playing right now." Another half a month passed, and Kong Qiu still hadn't learned any new pieces of music.

Finally, he felt something in the music and cried, "Who else can make such music other than the King Wen of Zhou!" Master Shi Xiang was shocked by his realization because the music was indeed composed by King Wen of Zhou.

People in Kong Qiu's time already celebrated the Spring Festival for New Year, and the State of Lu had spring worship ceremonies. Kong Qiu would celebrate the Spring Festival with his family, light lanterns, stay up for the night (*shousui*),* and tell his children stories about the festival. Kong Li liked to play with the *Nuo* opera masks or make funny faces to scare his little sister.

* Staying up for the night (*shousui*) on New Year's Eve is a folk tradition in China. *Shousui* starts with the New Year's Eve dinner, and people stay up all night to say goodbye to the old year and welcome the new year with hope and excitement.

People burned bamboo to welcome the new year, believing its cracking sound could expel all evil spirits or sicknesses. The ritual, as well as fireworks in later times, was called *baozhu*, "cracking bamboo." Kong Qiu and his family would burn the bamboo together at the Spring Festival, with the hope that the new spring would bring them better lives.

When he was thirty, Kong Qiu established his private school, which was groundbreaking at the time, and he became the first person to introduce education to the general public. Learning was exclusively designed for the nobilities during the Western Zhou period (1046–771 BCE). Kong Qiu changed this situation by raising the idea that "there should be no distinction of classes in teaching." Whoever had the aspiration to learn, despite birth and age, could become his student. He thus became known as Master Kong or Confucius.

Among his students were Yan Hui, who was thirty years younger, and Yan Hui's father, Yan Lu, who was only six years younger. There was Yuan Xian, who was too poor to have a proper home, and there was Bu Shang, who came from afar.

Confucius did not teach in a specific location. He would choose his classroom based on the number of students and weather, "Confucius, rambling in the forest of Zi-wei, stopped and sat down by the Apricot altar." On warm spring days, he and his students sat under the apricot blossom tree in the courtyard and talked about the Zhou Dynasty rituals and poems.

Later, the term *xingtan*, "apricot altar," was used to refer to education in general.

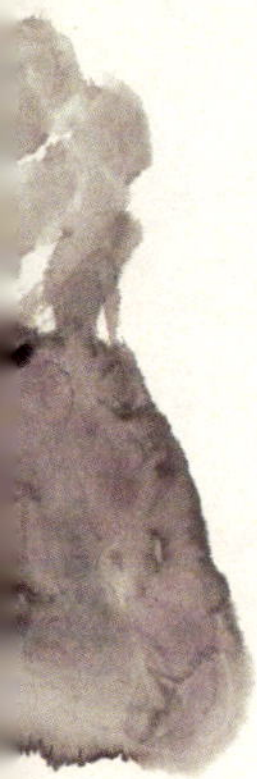

Confucius insisted on the principle of teaching in line with students' abilities and conducted individualized instruction for his many students based on their personalities. When Yan Hui and Fan Chi asked about the meaning of benevolence, his answers were different. When Ziyou and Zixia asked about the meaning of filial piety, his answers were also different. Confucius also required his students to be honest with their knowledge and understanding. "When you know a thing, to hold that you know it; and when you do not know a thing, to allow that you do not know it." This is still the learning principle that Chinese people follow today.

Confucius carried out his teaching through free discussions and debates, which was the most outstanding feature of *xingtan* education. The teacher and students could freely express their opinions on any topic, such as history, society, nature, and rituals.

In such ways, Confucius inspired his students' intelligence and helped them find truth without discrimination. Their talks were later compiled into a masterpiece of thought, *The Analects*.

During their free time, Confucius and his students often went for a bath and had fun at the Wuyu Altar by the River Yi, south of Qufu. One day, when they were there, Confucius asked his students to talk about their wishes and aspirations.

Zilu, Ran Qiu, and Gongxi Hua all shared in turns. Then, Zeng Dian said, "All I want is to bathe in the Yi River with my friends in spring, dance in the wind on the Wuyu Altar, and then happily sing and go home." Confucius heard and sighed, "You have articulated my wish!"

Confucius taught his students the Six Arts: rites, music, archery, charioteering, calligraphy, and mathematics. Many of his students, such as Zilu and Ran Qiu, were skillful chariot drivers.

When teaching about driving, Confucius said, “You must hold the reins with absolute concentration. You must not talk or gesture as you wish.”

Someone from Daxiang said, "Confucius knows everything, but unfortunately, he does not have a specialty that people know of."

Hearing this, Confucius answered with a smile, "What specialist should I be? Driver? Archer? I guess I will be a driver."

"People who want to be good chariot drivers need to know how to use the horses' strengths equally and together. They need to follow the horses' will whenever they are making a turn. That way, they will be able to drive on a chariot to places as far as they want." Confucius himself often traveled by chariot, and he enjoyed the feeling of riding in the wind.

Confucius was very fond of sports. When "Confucius shot arrows at Qufu, the onlookers surrounded him like a wall."

He said, "There is nothing that a gentleman should fight or compete for. If they do, it must be archery! The archers greet each other before the competition, and they drink to their hearts' delight afterward. It is such a noble competition!"

Confucius also often took his student Yan Hui for a walk. Sometimes, he walked fast, sometimes slow, and Yan Hui followed his pace.

This was Confucius showing his student, who was not very strong physically, how to exercise through hiking. Yan Hui also followed his master in his learning and life. Their stories were later known as "Yan following Kong's steps."

While many people know Confucius as the founder of Confucianism, few know that he was also a running enthusiast.

According to historical records, Confucius was passionate about running and ran like he could catch hares in the wilderness.

Confucius was also good at weightlifting. Just like his father, he could lift the huge bar that bolted the city gate with his hands.

During a battle, his father, Shuliang He, stopped the city gate from falling with his own hands so that the army of the Lu State could retreat. After that, he was known for his strength by everyone.

Confucius said, "Clever people like water, and benevolent people like mountains. Clever people are active, and benevolent people are calm. Clever people live happily, and benevolent people live long." He taught his students to be virtuous and respectful of nature. He is believed to be one of the first educators to integrate ecological morality into human ethics.

Confucius often took his students to the East Mountain (today's Yi Mountain, southeast of Zoucheng in Shandong Province). "There are many mountains surrounding the State of Lu, and the East Mountain is the most unique in its beauty and elegance."

Confucius and his students "ascended the East Mountain, and the State of Lu appeared to them small." They practiced rock climbing and hiking and enjoyed the beautiful scenery.

One day, the master and disciples went on a trip to Mount Tai. They supported each other up the high and steep mountain.

On the top of the mountain, they looked into the far distance and felt "all beneath the heavens appeared small."

Confucius often rowed boats in the Si River. Watching the rushing water, he felt that people's lives rushed forward just like the unstoppable river. He said, "It passes on just like this, not ceasing day or night!"

His philosophical understanding of water has since influenced Chinese culture for thousands of years.

On a sunny day, Confucius and his disciple Zilu went to the mountains. They saw some pheasants playing and foraging. Seeing people coming, they flew up, circled around in the air, landed again, and returned to their games. Confucius and Zilu were amazed by this interesting and peaceful sight, and they stopped to watch.

“These pheasants know their place and time well. They stay here because they understand no one will harm them,” said Confucius. Zilu bowed to the pheasants, which opened their wings and disappeared into the fog.

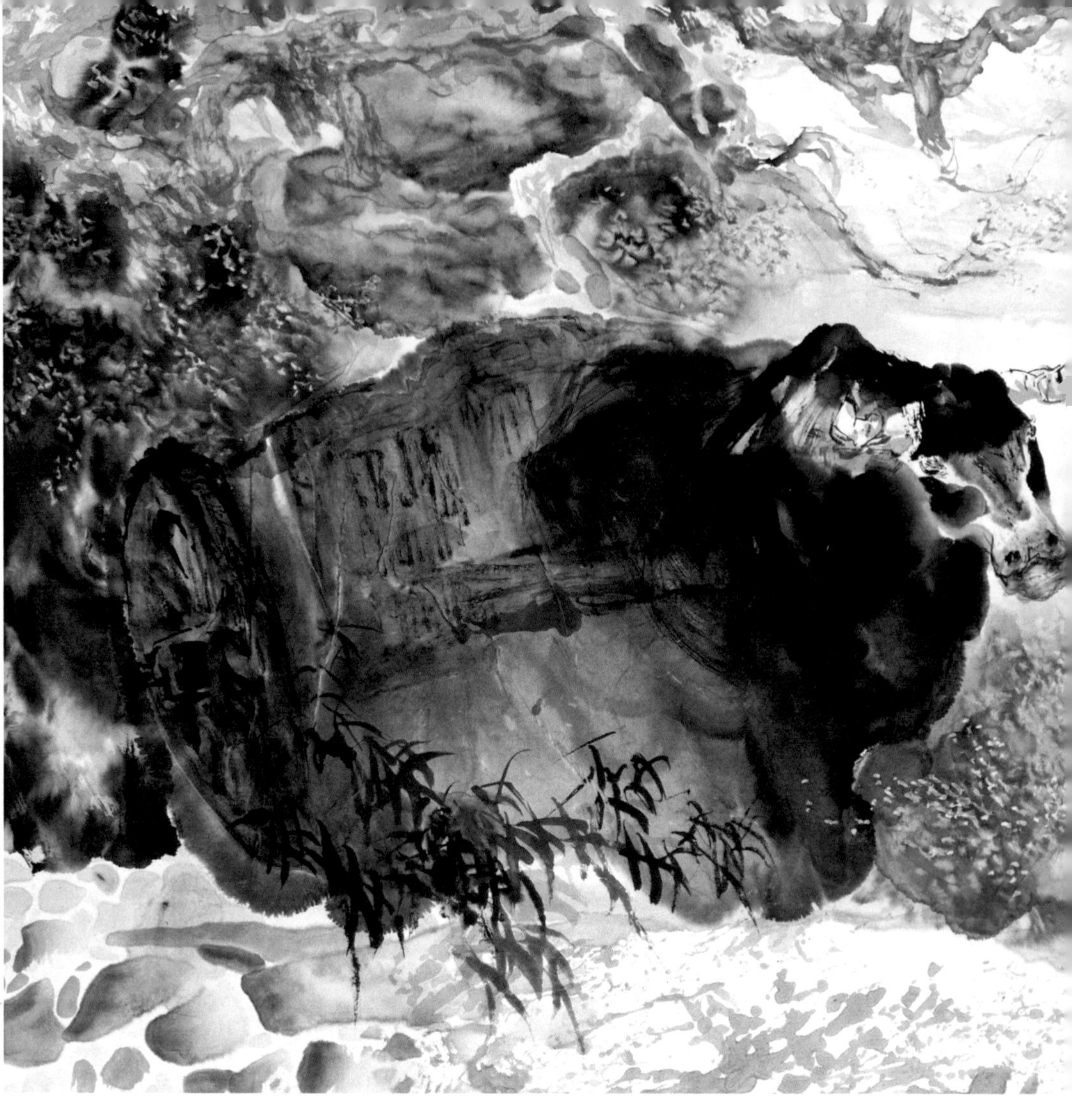

Confucius's disciple, Zizhang, asked, "How can a person be successful wherever he goes?"

Confucius answered, “If he is honest with his words and solemn and kind with his behavior, he can be successful even when he goes to the south and north borders. If he is not honest with his words and not solemn or kind with his behavior, can he be successful even when he stays in his local community?”

Zizhang thus invited his master to write this on his belt so that he could read it every day.

Confucius's friend Yuan Rang lost his mother and was too sad to arrange her funeral. Confucius generously offered to help. He selected the coffin and painted and decorated it himself. Yuan Rang, who should be expressing his grief, stepped onto his mother's coffin and began to sing. Seeing this, the neighbors all persuaded Confucius not to help this person anymore. But Confucius said, "He is my old friend. Let's still help him with the funeral for his mother's sake."

Confucius, now thirty-four years old, had always wanted to study with the "old master," Lao Tzu, who lived in Luoyi (today's Luoyang), the capital of the State of Zhou. It was too far from the State of Lu, and Confucius could not afford the travel expenses. His disciple Nangong Jingshu thus appealed to Duke Zhao of Lu about his master's wish, and the latter provided Confucius with two horses, a carriage, and a servant for his trip. Confucius said, "I hear Lao Tzu is very talented and well-learned. He knows the origin of rites and music and can tell the destination of morality and the Way. I will go to him today and be his student."

When he passed the Yellow River, Confucius shot down a wild goose as a present for Lao Tzu. After Lao Tzu heard about it, he came out to welcome Confucius in person.

Lao Tzu was then the imperial librarian of the State of Zhou. He carefully planned Confucius's study, asking him to read through the classics first and then discuss the Zhou rituals.

Under Lao Tzu's guidance, Confucius read the *Eulogy of Shang*, the *Eulogy of Zhou*, and over 3,000 classical texts. This prepared him for compiling the *Book of Documents*. He also carefully studied the *Rites of Zhou* and the official histories of several hundred feudal states, which prepared him for compiling the *Spring and Autumn Annals*.

During their time together, Confucius and Lao Tzu thoroughly discussed rites, morals, and other topics. In addition to the *Dao De Jing*, Lao Tzu also wrote some articles on "Towards the Origin of Rites and Music," but were not preserved. Fortunately, Lao Tzu taught all his works to Confucius, who mentioned the theory of "Towards the Origin of Rites and Music" in his own works. This prepared for the mutual integration of Confucian and Daoist cultures.

Lao Tzu also took Confucius to visit the Sacrificial Hall, the Imperial Ancestral Temple, and ceremonial places where the King offered sacrifices to Heaven and Earth "to observe the former King's regulations and learn about the summit of the rite and music system." As the place where the Kings of Zhou worshipped their ancestors and held court meetings, the Sacrificial Hall had nine *ding* vessels from the former dynasty and a portrait of the Duke of Zhou (Ji Dan, the son of King Wen of Zhou).

The Duke of Zhou was a saint in Confucius's heart. He stopped before his portrait for a long time and often dreamed of him after that.

Lao Tzu introduced Confucius to the musician Chang Hong, and the three talked about the Duke of Zhou's composition, *Da Wu,* and the cultural origin of music. *Da Wu* reflected the entire process of Zhou's unification and governance of the state and was considered the national music of the Zhou people.

The time Confucius had in Luoyi studying with Lao Tzu was the happiest of his life. He made discoveries and formed new thoughts almost every day, and he developed a profound relationship with Lao Tzu.

Before Confucius left, Lao Tzu told him, “I hear wealthy people give out money and benevolent people give out words. I am not wealthy, so I shall steal the title of a benevolent one and see you off with words.” Confucius carefully listened to what his master had to say and stood for a long time to see him off.

During his journey back to the State of Lu, his disciples asked, “What kind of person do you think Lao Tzu is?”

Confucius answered, “Birds in the sky can fly, animals on the ground can run, and fish in the water can swim. These I already know.”

"But how can I know anything about Chinese dragons? They come with the clouds and leave with the wind. They have so many forms, and no one can know them all. Lao Tzu is completely beyond my imagination. I think he is probably like a Chinese dragon."

There is a story about Confucius in the *Three Character Classic*, which said, "Zhongni used to study from Xiang Tuo."*

Once, when Confucius traveled to Zhongmu, he was stopped by a group of children who were building a miniature city with sand. Confucius got off the carriage and asked the children to make way.

---

* Xiang Tuo was a very smart child during the Spring and Autumn Period (770–476 BCE). Confucius had asked him some questions, and he was revered in later times as "Lord Sage."

One of the children, Xiang Tuo, asked him in return, "Carriages must go around the city wall; how can a city make way for the carriage?"

Confucius found little Xiang Tuo's argument reasonable and said, "The people here in Zhongmu can be taught. Even children can reason like this, not to mention the adults." He reversed his carriage and detoured around the children's game.

After he returned to the State of Lu, Confucius received more disciples.

Once, on a trip with Zilu and Yan Hui, Confucius asked them to talk about their aspirations.

Zilu said, "I wish to share all my carriages, horses, and furs with my friends and not regret it even if they are ruined this way."

Yan Hui said, "I wish to not brag about my efforts and achievements."

Zilu then asked about his master's aspiration.

Confucius said, "They are, in regard to the aged, to give them rest; in regard to friends, to show them sincerity; in regard to the young, to treat them tenderly."

Only by studying hard can one gain knowledge. This was what Confucius told his disciples. Among them, his favorite was Yan Hui. "Admirable indeed was the virtue of Hui! With a single bamboo dish of rice, a single gourd dish of drink, and living in a shabby lane, while others could not have endured the distress, he did not allow his joy to be affected by it."

Yan Hui came from a poor family, and he was one of Confucius's youngest disciples. However, he was very diligent and devoted to his studies. The later generations called him "Continuator of the Sage."

Confucius was thirty-five when the State of Lu was struck by a coup initiated by the three great clans, Jisun, Shusun, and Mengsun, which forced Duke Zhao of Lu to flee the country. Confucius was indignant by this disorder, and he left for the State of Qi.

At Linzi, the capital of Qi, Confucius heard the Shao Music (a traditional Chinese court music) and was deeply touched. He focused on learning to play and sing this music, forgetting all other physical enjoyment and not even thinking of eating meat for months. The Shao Music, also called Xiaoshao and Jiushao, was composed during the time of Emperor Shun and has nine sections. Confucius commented on it as "perfectly beautiful and also perfectly good."

"The Shao is the music left by Emperor Shun. It is gentle and peaceful like the south breezes blowing." The people of Qi praised Confucius for his extreme devotion and love for learning.

When Confucius and his friends got together and his friends sang a good song, Confucius would invite them to sing again while he himself followed them. He was always very happy to learn a good song.

ABOUT THE AUTHOR

Guo Defu is a famous contemporary Chinese ink-wash painter and representative artist of the Confucian school of painting. With an artistic career of nearly 60 years, he is renowned for his expertise in painting Chinese historical figures. His work, *The Painting Biography of Confucius*, has been exhibited in art exhibitions and book fairs in France, Belgium, Russia, Germany, Australia, Republic of Korea, the United States, and countries along the Belt and Road, allowing audiences from around the world to experience the spirit and charm of Confucius and traditional Chinese culture up close.